ALSO BY DANIEL SIMON

POETRY

After Reading Everything (2016)

Cast Off (2015)

∞

ANTHOLOGIES

Dispatches from the Republic of Letters: 50 Years of the Neustadt International Prize for Literature (2020)

Nebraska Poetry: A Sesquicentennial Anthology, 1867–2017 (2017)

UNDER A GATHERING SKY

Daniel Simon

STEPHEN F. AUSTIN STATE UNIVERSITY PRESS

For more information:
Stephen F. Austin State University Press
P.O. Box 13007 SFA Station
Nacogdoches, Texas 75962
sfapress@sfasu.edu

Production Manager: Kimberly Verhines
Cover Image: "Sandhills Reflections," © Michael Forsberg, michaelforsberg.com / Reproduced by permission

The title of the book, *Under a Gathering Sky,* comes from a phrase in Lucille Clifton's "The Photograph: A Lynching," in *Blessing the Boats* (2000). To learn more about Professor Clifton's legacy, visit thecliftonhouse.org.

ISBN: 978-1-62288-259-5

FIRST EDITION

Distributed by Texas A&M University Press Book Consortium / www.tamupress.com

To my wife and family—lambent, life-giving flames—
with love and profound gratitude.

⚮

CONTENTS

UNDER A GATHERING SKY

What is it to be estranged in this land? It is in the land, I once thought, that one searches out and eventually finds what is beautiful. And an edge of this deep and rarefied beauty is the acceptance of complex paradox and the forgiveness of others. It means you will not die alone.
— Barry Lopez, *Arctic Dreams* (1986)

∞

What do we know ourselves,
how do we remember,
and what is it we find in the end?
— W. G. Sebald, *Austerlitz* (2001)

∞

Either light exhilarates the watchful heart
That heeds its guidance
Or does not exist.
— Kebir Ammi, "The Old Man" (2021)

I AUGURIES

Declaration at the Border

Enter the new country, writes Nouwen.
The country of love.
The country of memory.
The country of crossing over.

Yet we linger on the border.
Does our Beloved dwell within or without?
Clinging tightly to ideas we once held, we cradle
them in our arms as we stand on the threshold.
At the checkpoint, fear screams at us to turn around.

The country of the future
doesn't care about our papers.
Nor does it matter what past we declare
or on whose authority we present ourselves.
The allegiances we claim will decide our fate.

Raising our hands, we profess what we believe
will permit us to pass. Yet the guard demands only
loyalty, not belief. Just beyond the edge of vision,
we declare something we cannot see
but one day hope to hold again.

Gathering

First the scattering, then the gathering.
In between — before mourning turns into joy —
the waiting. In exile, months turn into years,
memory of the homeland fades, the bonds of
kinship fray. When we hear the call of return,
at first we cannot bring ourselves to believe it:
in the valley, we fear, lies only death. Yet
to remain scattered surely means to perish.
Thus we cling to the promise of return —
invisible strands lead us upon the path,
guiding us when we no longer see the way.
Bolstering our resolve to press on.

The Banks of Time

after W. G. Sebald

Where the river narrows,
you are shot like a javelin
through the straits of mortality.

Paddles are useless here
as is the desperation
of looking back upstream

hoping to better prepare
for the turbulence to come
— or longing for time

to reverse its course.
If you make it through
the chute and are cast out

onto slack water, you swear
that time didn't slow down:
the javelin just picked up speed

as it arched downward, homing.

Stepwise

Ten thousand places:
each the destination of
ten thousand paces,
stepwise in pursuit
of wisdom yet blind
to what lies beyond
our line of sight —
what lies we tell our-
selves to muster the
courage to go on —
what truths, bounding
ahead of our next step,
are bound up in know-
ing when it's too late
to turn (our lives)
around

Scratch Poem

If you've got one, scratch it.
A verse or an itch, no matter.
It's what our animal selves would do.

Scraping in the dirt, like a chicken,
keeps the poem slightly sullied,
turns the eye from its pristine glare.

Lines of relief on a scratchboard surface
lend depth to the glassy sheen of vacancy.

Most lines are made from an impression
abraded on the slate façade of time,
arcs of light hurled against night's pitch.

Sharing the Pain

Old French compaignon,
'one who breaks bread with another'

The ship of companionship
has been quarantined, leaving
those aboard at the mercy of
the one who knows: only by saving
a remnant from this batch of dough
will the next day's leavening
be assured.

Residuals

When we sieve the year
to remove its impurities,
the dregs that remain
at the bottom of our cup
remind us: every elixir
begins with something
crushed.

Retrospection

Death is a string that binds together
the scattered beads of the universe.
— Ghalib

If dissolution is our fate, may my scattering
be bound up, not by death's garrote, but in
the hands of one who, tracing the path I've
traveled, picks up the beads fallen from my
pocket, unspooling as life's knot unraveled
behind me. When I turned around to tally
my loss, what I thought was intention
turned out to be some other's design.

Dry Cataract

The stump.

An inelegant word
and stubborn reminder —
we let the tree die.

The maple, under the double blow
of ice storm and suffocating drought,
conspiring to doom it to early demise.

Yet the unseen cause was soon revealed:
wire encaged the root ball like a manacle,
choking it in subterranean death.

On a day of autumnal equinox,
forces of light and dark in fleeting balance,
death lay, shackled, in deformation.

Imperceptibly, the light shifted
as I extricated the stump from its iron crown,
cascading black into the crater left behind.

Auguries of Incipience

after William Blake

Nature's every metaphor for
new beginnings implies a cycle,
not stepping over a threshold;
turn over a new leaf, and you
realize that calendars mimic
trees; see your daughter reach
for a fruit, and you know that
growth rings measure time's
concentric circles of *sweet delight*
and *Endless Night.* Lengthening
days replay each nocturne's fading
melody; sap rising from root to bole
augurs the ascendancy of rebirth.

Shadows on the Wall

If you turned around and peered into the fire,
would you prefer the shadows instead?
If they extinguished the flames,
would you favor smoke over shadow?
If the cave flooded with water,
would forms float to the surface?
If you could touch the wall of the cave,
would your fingertips trace what you saw,
caressing the face of knowledge?

Jupiter's Ear

Midway along life's path,
if ascent is still an option,

is it possible to spring
forth, fully formed,

before Minerva's owl
takes flight at sundown?

No dark wood surrounding
or night of the soul looming

just the concatenation
of storylines, irresolution

and serendipity accreting
into the lineation of days.

Not chaos theory
but a sort of indeterminacy

radical in implication —
neither fate nor absurdity

just reason enough to go on
despite all evidence to the contrary.

II DIALOGUES

Books I Haven't Read

The Book of the Dead	in proof stage
The Book of Life	already checked out
The Book of Nights	1,001 delights, but it doesn't end well
The Book of Sun and Shadow	the flesh made word (*see* Neruda)
The Book of Enlightenment	trapped in the body
The Book of the Body	thank God for that
The Book of Redemption	written in a foreign language
The Book of Childhood	erased by time's arrow
The Book of Happiness	shadows on the wall of the cave
The Book of Endings	turn back to page 1

The Archer's Hand

> *Let your bending in the archer's hand be for gladness.*
> —Kahlil Gibran

For life goes not backward
still we peer into the well's depths

as living arrows sent forth
we hone the tip to be razor-sharp,
hoping its pain will pierce the less

the mark upon the path
guides our footfalls to follow theirs,
but what landmarks guide us
when the path grows faint?

of the infinite
water reflects the sky's expanse,
while fractals trouble the polished surface
we'd hoped would mirror truth

He bends you
to the point of fracture
and then bends you further
past your tolerance to bear it

with His might
just when we think mercy
ought to temper might and
that mourning might end

the arrow that flies
indeed must pierce the mark
were it to pass through grief

the bow that is stable
pulls taut our unwindings

Too Much in the Sun

What is the measure of man?
A quintessence of dust,
scattered on the boards each day?

Yet shaken out, our dust
measures little more than
leaf mold, or fly ash,

an evanescence of smoke,
disintegrations of being —
fully human in the perishing.

Aubade

Do you not hear the nightingales call?
They understand the heart's yearning,
they know the pain of love.
— Ludwig Rellstab

The beloved always hearkens to birdsong
when love is most impossible, the lover's
yearning always broken like night's spell
betrayed by sunrise, as if the heart only
dreamt in color against a curtain of black.

Just when the first rays promise
to illuminate the one beside us,
song takes flight

                outside our window.

Bloodstone

I on the edge / of Empire walking west
— Gerald Stern

Where once lapped an inland Permian sea
now only a reflecting pool remains,

Chinese pistache, amur maple, eastern redbud
rise up in mute sentience out of mineral-red dirt,

leaves tipped in shades of scarlet, burnt orange, Tyrian purple
against trunks blackened in funereal suits of mourning.

Looking up to read an inscription above the archway,
words resist being spoken aloud, yet a hand on the shoulder

steadies our ascent. I do not guide but only follow
as we enter through a small portal into autumn sunlight.

Pines like sentries mark the threshold where we cross over
to rows of empty chairs, frozen in a moment of time,

radiant with brass yet cold to the hand, resting on glass
like blocks of sculpted ice in translucent witness.

We ascend another slope past hematite-stained stone
to circle the great elm, scarred by a concussive wind

that leaves twin trunks bowed down in unison,
less in supplication than resilient endurance.

Descending, we circle back to where we began
and head west along the water's edge,

in empire's wake, two hand-in-hand,
two still behind, as water drops down

to depths unfathomed in a vanished sea.

Keeping Grace

after Gerard Manley Hopkins

For that I came: water-borne, lit by the flame
that my godparents held in their hands
at my baptism, not knowing their own
candle would be quenched too soon

For that I came: whose being in flight
on those swings, sunlight and the wind's
whoosh in my ears, nature's sonnet *flinging
out broad its name,* sounding echoes in return

For that I came: to discover in library stacks
ten thousand places whose ciphered names
I whispered aloud to see if they might reveal
the shadow and light contained within

For that I came: to blow on the embers of such
grace in my hands, to be washed in that font
which *speaks and spells* what I'm meant to be,
to be drawn into that lambent, life-giving flame

Scales I

> *Everyone their own devastation. Each on its own scale.*
> —Robert Hass

We were not put on earth . . . to express ourselves.
But were we put on earth . . . to be forced into silence?

Some of us whispered 'art'
Those who still believe in art   even when haunted
by devastation   devastation   devastation

Some of us 'truth'
Which depends on whether the truth of art resides
in self-expression or in its mirror held up to reality

A debate with cut vocal chords
So we read Philomela's tapestry instead —
each thread its own chord, vocalized

Truth, of course, was death.
Art, of course, would reverse death's truth
by sublimating time's limit into revelation

Silence precedes us. We are catching up.
Yet expression holds silence at bay
or pauses to let silence have its say

There is silence at the end, and it doesn't explain.
Silence, by definition, defies explanation.
Meaning, by extension, reconnects the chords.

Making

Alma, Colorado

Aspen leaves, wind-frenzied, dance.
Pine boughs sway in soporific assent.
It's the sunlight, of course, that delights
the eye as much as the wind, that move-
ment of *finches' wings* which Hopkins
delected: all *dappled* and *stippled* and *plotted*
and *pieced.* One verb *fathers-forth* the rest
of the poem, a litany of participles and
adjectives towed along in creation's wake,
our grammar of assent in two imperatives,
and *praise*, finally, but less for the creator
than for the manifold: like the magpie that
delights in versicoloring, *pied beauty*
also our trade: taking the *who knows how?*
as our dazzlement by change, our challenge
not to lament but praise, to be delighted and
stippled and chastened as we, too, are makers.

The Iniquity of Oblivion

after W. G. Sebald

Lest thou forget, like the proverbial
sands of time, sifts through our
fingertips the more we clutch at
its decree, that litany of *nots*
like the tolling threat of ruin.

Yet to be punished for time's
attrition — must we be lashed
for some unmerited culpability?
When time *blindly scatters her
poppyseed*, why not flower, too,

in the scattering? Or rather,
grant us that Lethean calyx,
turn oblivion into oblation,
pour the elixir into your hands,
rub it, again, into my dimming eyes.

Word Matters

Eliot's words slipped and slid, did not *stay in place*.
These words sluice in channels, invisible embankments
that shore up the extravagances of thought.
As the porte-parole of tongues,
what carries the weight of weightlessness?
Embarking on a skiff, they pole their way downstream,
hoping to arrive at the source, to shed the ropes
mooring them
        to meaning.

Blackbird's Lament

every step you take is guided by | The love of
the light on the land and the blackbird's cry
— Jane Siberry

You propitiate those who wound you the most
yet believe those wounds are self-begotten.
Punishing your body, you spurn that most precious
gift even as you empty out your very being
for the sake of their happiness.

The pallor of your heart's lamentation
settles like gray fog in the valley, yet your
painterly eye delights in the *light on the land,*
and the peaks themselves self-array in splendor.

Scales II

> *. . . its pinnacle to heavenward*
> —Robert Frost

Questions of scale
Ladders of ascension
Mote-obscuring vision
Clambering vine of the mind
Bark that sheathes heartwood
Branches bowsprung heavenward
Vault of sky arced in transcendence
Scale scraped away with dull knives
Expectations tamped into the dirt
Still *stiff and sore and scarred,*
To earthward we turn,
Pinnacles enfolded,
Plummeting

Final Harvest

after Emily Dickinson

Upwellings of the heart —
like tectonic clouds that

uplift and gather — pulse until
the Heaves of Storm subside

Those sheaves not brought into
the barn evade the threshing time —

that whip of lightning, one last
flaying of the mortal coil

Gathering Calm

The house was quiet
and the world was calm.
— Wallace Stevens

That would be bliss
a reader and a book
a communion of words
a mind cleared
of all dross and distraction.

But the world stops by
for a visit — unbidden
yet persistent. Surcease
would mean blood
gelled in place, thought
stilled in abstraction,
body held in abeyance.

Lines of sight
always refract what
demands to be seen,
memory's junk drawer
spilled out across
the floor of consciousness.

A quiet house gathers
the ashes of emotion
then sweeps them away
in gusts of time.

Not Another Poem about Poetry

Just another verse taking up
words in the mind
lines on a page
pages in a book
books on a shelf
shelves upon shelves
like overlapping waves
not quite straight but curved
drawing the gloaming horizon over itself
patterned against shadows on the mind's canvas
small constellation of making, unmaking, making anew

III INGATHERING

Under a Gathering Sky

after Lucille Clifton

If we are *required to view it together*
through *cut glass* eyes, what story
would the *accurate album* tell?

If textbooks whitewash history,
and the dead tell true tales, what
manifests: destiny or complicity?

Pictures in an album construct narratives
less about accuracy than sudden
flashes of truth, less about gathering

than frames cutting into pieces
our witnessing, such skies that cry out,
WERE YOU NOT THERE WITH BLOOD ON YOUR HANDS?

Miss Flannery Regrets

If a writer's diet seems strange,
we like to think the strangeness
of her stories somehow derives
from such odd dining tastes:
pineapple with mayonnaise,
spam with rusk, a tablespoon
of rotgut mixed with water
(to help her sleep, of course).

In those daily letters to Regina,
filled with gossip and endearments,
novenas and social engagements,
Mary Flannery becomes Miss Flannery
before our eyes. Even when *nothing much
doing around here* is her refrain, the writer
gradually asserts control over the minutiae
of her routine, the daughter gently but firmly
reproving the mother.

                    And the *nothing much*,
we realize, is a smokescreen behind which
the labor of the writer insists, most of all,
on shutting out the world while mastering
its craft, craft held up to a crooked
mirror, in praise of its follies.

Lumpen Literati

swindlers, confidence tricksters, brothel-keepers,
rag-and-bone merchants, beggars, and other flotsam . . .
— Karl Marx

The refuse of all classes, wrote Marx,
rogues, rascals, and reprobates,

unreliable servants to the revolution
like those writers and artists lumped together

and jettisoned into the dustbin of history,
the first time as tragedy, the second time as farce.

Let us mince them in a farce, shall we,
and stuff them ass-backwards

into a carcass, a force-meat of poetry,
embalmed in rhetorical eloquence,

and roast them in an oven, well basted,
lest they gurgitate, yet again.

[Reframe]

l'absente de tous bouquets
— Stéphane Mallarmé

Of all the pictures in the album you made me,
the missing photo is one that reframes all
the rest: the absent flower, in the bouquet of
stems plucked from their bed, the one that
absented me from you. Yet without those
blank pages at the end, would I have known to write
on them in a language you could not understand?
Outside the frame, do I remember what I
wish you would have said at that moment?
The album: that fallow ground of perpetuity.

Days of Reckoning

after Rea Baldridge's Ride of the Obliterati

Whited out, disappeared, disremembered —
a national reign of obliteration would
blot our collective memory were it not for
the storykeepers who keep the true oath:
to bear witness to *that which happened.*

Yet horsemen rein apocalyptic steeds across
desolate landscapes, brandishing weapons while
trampling bodies underfoot, as helicopters
tighten their noose around strays who might
make a break to escape the killing fields.

Hemmed in and assaulted by endless video loops
and brawling screeds, does our field of vision exceed
the mind's capacity to order the overwhelming chaos?
to make sense of what we see? We lay down stories
like breadcrumbs that others might retrace our paths.

Words, too, beckon like crumbs, and we trust that
brushstrokes, leading the eye into the maelstrom,
might give us moments of respite in small eddies of
calm: semaphores of hope, testaments of balladeers,
sentinels that keep watch lest democracy die.

A Little Dream That Died

after Louisa Brooke

The daughter of an Episcopalian bishop, she led
a life of quiet desperation in a college town,
surrounded by people in their *little gossip-hells*.
A *sometime Adviser of Women* and teacher of English
with a degree from Vassar, what fate led her
back to the Southern Plains in her twenties?

In those years before the Great War, she nursed
her literary ambitions in a *heap of ruin* for a house,
despising her landlord (and no doubt her fellow tenants)
while looking out from an attic window and biding her
time between teaching and giving etiquette lessons.

When the war started, she took an unpaid leave of
absence and moved back east, where she met and
married a maritime attorney. They eventually made
the society pages of the *Times*.

She collected rare books and art and raised her daughters
to be cultured and refined, but the dream that died in that
college town died a second time when she became
a young bride, when the *little oil* in her literary lamp
flickered out.

Spotted

When we see something, suddenly, why do we say we *spotted* it?
Is it like a spot on the rug that catches our eye in passing,
or the pupil projecting itself on the blank screen of the
    unexpected?
Blood and ink spots, the patterning of snake, turtle, trout, and peacock,
the eye casts dispersion on the whole cloth of perception.
Some stain, or speck, or mote always floats or settles on the mind's
    canvas.
A spotlight to focus the attention, a blot that interrupts fixation,
a taint that stains innocence with meaning.

The Cloak of Sonship

When I was twenty-five,
I spent the summer back home
on the farm, after my first year
of grad school, having recrossed
the plains from Indiana to Nebraska.
Had my mom asked me to come home?
Was it just to find a job for the summer?
In my mind, I was the dutiful son,
but in my actions, was I the prodigal?
Is *riotous living* always the prelude to homecoming?

As the middle of five boys, I didn't quite fit
the parable: my older brothers had already
fulfilled the roles of elder and younger sons,
so I had to play a different part. How did I not
imagine a different ending? And why does
the mother fade from the story?

As my dad got sicker
that summer, he started sleeping
in the living room, too frail to climb the stairs.
He would have taught me how to kill the fatted calf.
My youngest brother, sixteen, still lived at home,
so I must have been jealous over how easy
I thought he had it, how spoiled he seemed to be.
I envied the best robe on his shoulders.

In August, I said goodbye to my father.
He seemed so thin and weak on that white sheet
on the pull-out couch, my grandmother already
too weak to hold him like a *pietà*.
Then I drove back to Indiana, alone.

Two weeks later, when my mom called
in the middle of the night,
I knew she was calling me home.
When we lowered his body into the dirt,
I couldn't see past that rough benediction:
the robe of bereavement cloaked us all.

Times Signature

Two-two
Unbuckle your belt
Four-four
Slam the door
Three-four
Pick up switch
Six-eight
Love in hate

Must be done
So drummer son
(Third in line)
Knows proper time
Learned by rote —
Let not the mote
Spare the child

Loose the wild
No mercies mild

Recipe

1½ cups of coffee
(in the morning)
¼ cup of milk per cup
1½ teaspoons of sugar
enough to start the day

½ a life at 44
¾ of my father's life
(dead at 58)
was it the proverbial
½ a pack a day that killed him?

measure for measure —
120/80 the ideal heart
20/20 the perfect sight
24/7 the daily grind
a grim calculus of attainment
the glaring objectivity
of quotas and deadlines

fractions that parse a life
whether wracked by weight
or by volume
no formula for a soul
no blueprint for dwelling
no map of the distances
between our habitations
at the same address

Song for My Father's Father

after Horace Silver

He listened to opera in a tie and overalls,
according to family lore, some Sunday-
afternoon respite from the weeklong
toil of farming. Did his parents bring
such cultural touchstones with them
to buff a veneer of sophistication
over their Czech peasant roots?
If polkas and waltzes got their
feet moving, opera and jazz moved
mind and heart. Whether orchestra
or combo, aria or shuffle, radio drama
or prized Victrola, the afternoon breeze
carried notes across the cornfields, a
sip of beer or wine lulling the listener
into a mellow mood, that trace of dirt
under fingernails: reminder
of Monday's chores to come.

Intertemporal Memo

Note to self RE: writing —
what seems legible today
is only so to this set of eyes.

In twenty years, will that
residue of today's trace still
be trailing blank across the page?

What forgetting will blanch the ink of witness,
what will the gust of intervening years efface?
Crossed out, will these lines still bleed through the chosen ones?

Does a memo exist only in transit?
Are we the recipient of our own TO: lines?
Dazzled by the deception of FROM: ?

Time | | Immemorial

September 11, 2021

Those who remember that day
always mention the blueness of the sky
that morning, as if to underscore
our collective innocence, as if two
of those three numerals already
anticipated the human will to counter
implacable gravity's grievous toll.

Yet words unscroll in waves horizontal,
wresting time's arrow from the
abysses   of space, reminding us that
that gap between | and | is all we are given
to nurture *in the land of the living*, that
tensile arc always lifting our feet from
the ground, suspending our fixity —

not an instant frozen in time but
eternity measured in grief-stricken-
ness, the living brought down to the
land of the dead — who remind us
to resume the ascent, to exhume meaning
from the rubble at our feet, to pry apart those
1's just far enough to let others pass through.

IV QUARTERINGS

Imponderables

Ils la portaient alternativement.
— Gustave Flaubert

The weight of the Baptist's head,
like the writer's burden of reality,
we shift from hand to hand
just to carry on

Not If, But When

The *whether* tricks us into thinking
it might or it might not happen
but why does the *when* always
stun us with its inevitability?

Not What, But How

When it comes down to a single question:
not *what are you going to do with your life,*
but why does it matter, and how will you
find strength for the journey?

Eight-Legged Shadow

I

Not arachnid
but double quadruped

Stilt-like two-footed
biped in pursuit

II

Magic-lantern striding
perpetual-motion gaited

Ratamacue of footfall —
luminescence, syncopated

Floodgate

The chute like a fall,
not from grace, but into fullness,
sluiced-out calcifications of thirst
— Augean stable of the mind —

Discipline

If true wisdom
comes from knowledge of death
then we are all students
of mortification

Reascent

In this purgatorio
side by side from the depths

a third one between us

V MIGRATIONS

Transmigration

Traversing the Great Plains south to north
in autumn, it's as if we are wading upstream
against the great migratory flows heading
south. The rivers, too, flow east and south,
heedless of human intention. What names
we give to the land will likewise be erased
by time's prevailing winds. What desire
we send forth — beating, beating, beating.

Sangre de Cristo

We crest Poncha Pass, heading southward,
the western flank of the Sangre de Cristos
like a View-Master panorama on our left.

Tracking the Rio Grande rift, we plunge into
the Spanish Southwest, where snakes turn
into *culebras* coiled around our feet.

Near Salida, a downburst of hail, stark white,
drifts across the two-lane highway and
assails the implacable, untouchable summits.

At Alamosa we turn east, pivot around Blanca Peak,
then pass through San Luis but do not mount
the stations of the cross alongside the way.

Crossing into New Mexico, we encounter Red River,
el río colorado. Did the river run red from blood or soil?
On foot, we navigate our ascent to the source.

Later, expelled to the east, the landscape levels out
to endless prairies, the inexorable pull toward the Gulf
sweeps us along over earth stained red

in the wake of prehistoric seas. Those blood-tinted peaks
left behind for flatlands where red silts down
in dry beds, scripted with other meanings.

Flying Homeward

for Dave (1964–2016)

To survive life on a northern plain
we presume strength is the most vital
rudiment, yet men who traverse the fields
are like those lonesome dreamers who witness
the great migrating flocks and abandon their
implements to pursue them in flight.

What spell comes over those not content to till the fields —
is it just a taste for meat, or does some hunter-gathering
atavism in the blood thrill to the chase, the sure shot,
the lifelike deceptions that would fill our pots with
muscle and marrow and not just a mess of pottage.

On your last hunt, the tableau of that predawn light
must have offered an incipient kaleidoscope of color,
a hushed moment anticipating the lone goose calling its brethren.
Like Jacob bowing before Esau, I ask for your blessing, not your
birthright, not your favorite gun but your favorite pen,

a leaning fence post to straighten between us,
some sagging barbed wire to tighten until it sings,
the smell of fresh-cut bales in a stifling hayloft,
skim ice on the pond reflecting infinite passing V's,
an Elysian field where we might walk together again.

"Blot out my transgressions"

sings the psalmist,
that the bones which thou
hast broken may rejoice.
The blows that splinter our
bones are visited upon the
perpetrator as much as
the innocents.

Such biblical transgressions blot
both the naked stain itself and
the pooling blood that spills
from the wound.

The bilabial *b*, deriving
from the Phoenician word
for *house*, is buffeted by the wind
sweeping across the mind's prairie,

white as snow. Leaning into the storm,
the words we speak ricochet backwards,
the house creaks and groans like a ship's timbers,
clouds spread their black sails like ink
towards the horizon.

(Dale) Hollow Still Life

All upright, as if standing at attention,
small pieces of slate align with astonishing
symmetry, no longer submerged and at the
waves' mercy, yet as if, somehow, in motion still.
Fibonacci-patterned like the whorls of a stone flower,
bereft of the water's nurturing arrangements,
desiccated yet in exquisite alignment — waiting for
waves to return and caress their patient longing,
waiting for eyes to witness their gray-robed petition,
waiting for ears to hear their slate-tongued colloquy.

Plumage

Cleaved together, two wings
enfold as if stilled in flight.
In free fall, concealed within them
the moment of their unfolding.
Feathered yet unfettered in descent,
like the plummeting of consciousness.

The Old Tree

No floodplain or swamp sits nearby.
Yet the river birch sends down roots
to tap some underground reserve of
moisture, then flings its catkins with
abandon into spring's bacchanalian wind.

Last year's October ice storm coated
branches and loitering leaves;   caught
unprepared, the birch split and splayed,
shackled by the thick ice coating as
branches convulsed, cascading down.

Then April's hail ball-peened the bark,
cankering its papery skin with thousands
of bruises, like the frail man who wraps his
threadbare blanket against the howling sleet,
swooning in a delirium of defenselessness.

With deep misgiving, I cut the birch down.

Sunflare

An arc of water inscribes the myth of eternal return.
A blackbird disappears and reappears, stilled in flight
even as the water in which it alights continues to flow.

The boy's pitcher endlessly refills and spills forth
to replenish the basin, as four winged lions stand at mute attention
while ancient oak leaves shade them in tranquility.

The yellow-breasted meadowlark flirts
with the water's edge but flares at the first hint of danger,
taking wary refuge from a vantage on high.

The blackbird dips in and out of view.
A blue jay — or is it gray? — peers at the boy, sipping from his pitcher.
The lark never returns. The water, unceasing, flows.

Pavane for a Dry Season

The dyad of my steps
patterns the couplets

of my thoughts: nascent,
falling; swelling, diminuendo.

Each two-step of desire
rolled back by lengthening

nights, each thirst a fermata
resolved by memory's mists.

Field Notes

Walking the rows from left to right,
right to left, each traversing seems to undo
the one that came before it. Reading from
left to right, left to right, what feels like
shackling oneself to the line instead liberates
the mind as the eye harvests by gathering word
by word. In the threshing that follows, letters fall
to the floor as the mind extracts the ripened grain
of meaning, golden light refracts flecks of dust,
and shadows pattern across the page. You raise
your eyes and look at me side to side, roll-casting
your gaze across the room to see if I might be
seduced by your meaning
seduced by your meaning.

After Rereading Everything

That shelf of books along the wall
looks quite different in middle age
— *nel mezzo del cammin* and all that —

than it did in my twenties when I
only began to realize how little I'd
ever read. Having gone down that

path more than double the length,
I know, now, that the measure of
purgatory is not so much in the steep

ascent that still lies ahead than in
the temptation to look back on all
the books I'll never read. The self-

winnowing shelf jettisons the books
that cause it to sag. The spines of
all the rest stand a little straighter,

knowing that the winnowing still
to come will happen in the thin air
where step labors to follow step.

Knowing

Starting at the base,
we keep climbing upward
even though we don't quite
know where the summit lies —
or whether we even have the
strength to attain it. Just when
the temptation to stop is greatest,
and turning around is the relief we
crave most, pressing on presupposes
belief more than knowledge, belief
that in knowing we will have
surpassed our limits, a new
perspective, beyond
knowing,
awaits.

Untidy Sonnet

Five fallow years,
that accumulation of blanks

Seasons of dread
marked by suspended resolution

Hesitant to plant
in last year's ashfall barrens

Yet seeding requires
imagining one's empty sack full

And till harvest we till
following each row as it leads us

Tending a mind
sprawled beyond its edges

Untidy sonnet,
strange marvel of fruitfulness

Acknowledgments

I'm grateful to Kimberly Verhines and the staff of Stephen F. Austin State University Press for the care with which they have handled this project.

With special thanks to Darlington Chibueze Anuonye, Rachel Tzvia Back, Anna Badkhen, David Baker, Lauren Camp, Alice-Catherine Carls, Robert Hass, Steve Langan, Ryan Long, Tess O'Dwyer, Rhona Seidelman, and Ted Kooser.

For the epigraph from Kebir Ammi's "The Old Man," thanks to Alice-Catherine Carls for co-translating the poem with me, which first appeared in *World Literature Today* and was reprinted in *Le vieil homme* (Éd. Al Manar, 2021).

Thanks to Liz Blood, who commissioned "Days of Reckoning" for *Art Focus Oklahoma* magazine's "Ekphrasis" column (January 2022).

At *Harvard Review*, thanks to Major Jackson, Chloe Garcia Roberts, and Cecilia Weddell for publishing " 'Blot out my transgressions' " (June 2022).

Thanks to Nathan Gunter and Karlie Ybarra for accepting "Field Notes" for the November 2022 issue of *Oklahoma Today*.

"Not If, But When," "Not What, But How," "(Dale) Hollow Still Life," and "Time || Immemorial" appear in *Voices Now: World Poetry Today*, edited by Braja K. Sorkar and Binay Laha (Tristoop Books, 2022).

Sources

3   Henri Nouwen, "Enter the New Country," in *The Inner Voice of Love* (1996)

5   W. G. Sebald, *Austerlitz*, trans. Althea Bell (2001)

10 Ghalib, "The Candle That Has Gone Out," in *The Lightning Should Have Fallen on Ghalib*, trans. Sunil Dutta & Robert Bly (1999)

12 William Blake, "Auguries of Innocence" (1803)

18 Kahlil Gibran, *The Prophet* (1923)

19 "A quintessence of dust" comes from act 2, scene 2 of *Hamlet*

20 Ludwig Rellstab, "Ständchen," adapted by Franz Schubert, *Schwanengesang*, D 957, no. 4

21 Gerald Stern, "The Same Moon above Us," in *Paradise Poems* (1984)

22 Gerard Manley Hopkins, "As Kingfishers Catch Fire" (1877)

23 Robert Hass, "Interrupted Meditation," in *Sun under Wood* (1996)

24 Gerard Manley Hopkins, "Pied Beauty" (1877)

25 W. G. Sebald, *The Rings of Saturn*, trans. Michael Hulse (1998)

26 T. S. Eliot, "Burnt Norton" (1936), in *Four Quartets*

27 Jane Siberry, "The Valley," in *Bound by the Beauty* (1989)

28 Robert Frost, "To Earthward," in *New Hampshire* (1923) and "The Silken Tent," in *A Witness Tree* (1942)

29 Emily Dickinson, "I heard a Fly buzz — when I died" (1862)

30 Wallace Stevens, "The House Was Quiet and the World Was Calm," in *Transport to Summer* (1947)

35 Lucille Clifton, "The Photograph: A Lynching," in *Blessing the Boats* (2000)

36 Flannery O'Connor, *Dear Regina: Flannery O'Connor's Letters from Iowa* (2022)

37 Karl Marx, *The Eighteenth Brumaire of Louis Bonaparte* (1852)

38 Stéphane Mallarmé, *Divagations* (1897)

40 Louisa Brooke, "Brick Dust," *Poetry* (1920)

45 Horace Silver, "Song for My Father," in *Song for My Father* (1963)

51 Gustave Flaubert, "Hérodias," in *Trois Contes* (1877)

ABOUT THE AUTHOR

A poet, translator, and essayist, Daniel Simon is assistant director and editor in chief of *World Literature Today* at the University of Oklahoma, where he also serves on the English, International Studies, and Judaic Studies faculty. The author of two previous verse collections, his poems have appeared in three anthologies, been translated into five languages, and nominated for multiple awards. *Nebraska Poetry: A Sesquicentennial Anthology, 1867–2017*, which he edited, won a 2018 Nebraska Book Award and was included on NPR's "50 States" summer booklist (2022). His latest anthology, *Dispatches from the Republic of Letters: 50 Years of the Neustadt International Prize for Literature* (2020), was a *Publishers Weekly* starred pick. Most recently, he served as consulting editor for the *Best Literary Translations* annual anthology, published by Deep Vellum in 2024. He is a member of the Academy of American Poets, PEN America, Nebraska Center for the Book, and the Norman Arts Council Roundtable. He and his wife have three daughters and live in Norman, Oklahoma.